Cronin

Native Americans

# Modoc

## Barbara A. Gray-Kanatiiosh

ABDO Publishing Company

# visit us at
# www.abdopublishing.com

Published by ABDO Publishing Company, 4940 Viking Drive, Edina, Minnesota 55435. Copyright © 2007 by Abdo Consulting Group, Inc. International copyrights reserved in all countries. No part of this book may be reproduced in any form without written permission from the publisher. The Checkerboard Library™ is a trademark and logo of ABDO Publishing Company.

Printed in the United States.

Cover Photo: Marilyn "Angel" Wynn/Nativestock.com
Interior Photos: Corbis pp. 4, 29; Nativestock.com p. 30; NSBO/www.byways.org p. 30
Illustrations: David Kanietakeron Fadden pp. 7, 9, 11, 13, 15, 17, 19, 21, 23, 25, 27
Editors: Rochelle Baltzer, Megan Murphy
Art Direction & Maps: Neil Klinepier

**Library of Congress Cataloging-in-Publication Data**

Gray-Kanatiiosh, Barbara A., 1963-
  Modoc / Barbara A. Gray-Kanatiiosh.
    p. cm. -- (Native Americans)
  Includes bibliographical references and index.
  ISBN-10 1-59197-656-1
  ISBN-13 978-1-59197-656-1
  1. Modoc Indians--Juvenile literature. 2. Indians of North America--Oregon--Juvenile literature. 3. Indians of North America--California--Juvenile literature. I. Title. II. Series: Native Americans (Edina, Minn.)

E99.M7G7 2006
979.4004'97412--dc22

                                                                    2004047793

## About the Author: Barbara A. Gray-Kanatiiosh, JD
Barbara Gray-Kanatiiosh, JD, Ph.D. ABD, is an Akwesasne Mohawk. She resides at the Mohawk Nation and is of the Wolf Clan. She has a Juris Doctorate from Arizona State University, where she was one of the first recipients of ASU's special certificate in Indian Law. Barbara's Ph.D. is in Justice Studies at ASU. She is currently working on her dissertation, which concerns the impacts of environmental injustice on indigenous culture. Barbara works hard to educate children about Native Americans through her writing and Web site, where children may ask questions and receive a written response about the Haudenosaunee culture. The Web site is: www.peace4turtleisland.org

## About the Illustrator: David Kanietakeron Fadden
David Kanietakeron Fadden is a member of the Akwesasne Mohawk Wolf Clan. His work has appeared in publications such as *Akwesasne Notes*, *Indian Time*, and the *Northeast Indian Quarterly*. Examples of his work have also appeared in various publications of the Six Nations Indian Museum in Onchiota, NY. His work has also appeared in "How the West Was Lost: Always the Enemy," produced by Gannett Production, which appeared on the Discovery Channel. David's work has been exhibited in Albany, NY; the Lake Placid Center for the Arts; Centre Strathearn in Montreal, Quebec; North Country Community College in Saranac Lake, NY; Paul Smith's College in Paul Smiths, NY; and at the Unison Arts & Learning Center in New Paltz, NY.

# Contents

# Where They Lived

The Modoc (MOH-dahk) originally called themselves *Maklak*, which means "the people" in their language. They spoke a **dialect** of the Penutian language family.

The tribe lived in parts of present-day Oregon and California. Modoc homelands were located within the northeastern part of the Modoc **Plateau**. This is near Lost River, Tule Lake, and Modoc Lake. The Klamath, Achomawi, and Shasta tribes lived nearby.

Modoc territory contained a variety of landforms. Some areas were mountainous. **Buttes**, ridges, and lava plateaus covered other parts. Lakes, rivers, streams, and wetlands also spread across the area.

Various plants and animals lived on Modoc land. Pine, fir, and oak

Today, people visit the Tule Lake National Wildlife Refuge in northern California. This area is part of Modoc homelands.

forests covered much of the territory. Juniper, sagebrush, and rabbitbrush grew along the edges of the forests. Elk and deer roamed these wooded areas. **Tule**, shrubs, and willows grew in abundance near the streams and the rivers. Every year, salmon swam up the rivers from the Pacific Ocean to lay their eggs.

**Modoc Homelands**

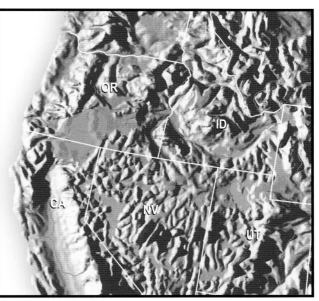

# Society

The Modoc were seminomadic. This means that they traveled in groups to follow animal **migrations**. But they also grew some crops. This provided their tribe with enough food.

Groups of Modoc lived in large villages. Each village owned certain lands for hunting, fishing, and gathering. When following animal migrations, the groups traveled within their specific areas. But, each group always returned to its main village for the winter.

Each Modoc village had leaders called *la gis*. The tribe elected la gis based on their speaking and judgment skills. La gis were respected for their wisdom, and they often taught children about morality. They were also expert hunters and warriors.

La gis were responsible for organizing trades and fulfilling the needs of their village. They also aimed to maintain peace both within the tribe and with outsiders. La gis had subleaders to assist them.

Usually, each village also had one shaman, or medicine person. This person healed others, interpreted dreams, and performed ceremonies. Like la gis, shamans were very much respected in Modoc society. And, sometimes they even became la gis.

Modoc permanent villages consisted of large groups of families. The families lived in underground homes.

# Food

The Modoc were hunters, fishers, and gatherers. Men were responsible for hunting and fishing. They hunted mule deer, elks, bighorn sheep, and antelope with bows and arrows. They used traps to hunt smaller animals such as rabbits, beavers, and otters. To catch birds, a hunter used a tool called a bola.

Men fished in the rivers. They stood along the riverbanks, or paddled into the river in rafts or canoes. The men caught many types of fish, including salmon and chub. They used spears, nets, or traps. Most commonly, they used a woven, cone-shaped trap. The men put fish eggs inside the trap to lure the fish. When a fish entered the larger end of the trap, it was unable to swim out.

While the men hunted and fished, Modoc women gathered wild fruits, plants, and seed. They collected acorns, chokecherries, **tule**, pine nuts, and water lily seed. They used sticks to pull up cattail roots and camas bulbs.

When men arrived home, women prepared and cooked their catches. The Modoc often ate fresh food, but they also dried some in the sun. Usually, they saved the dried food for the winter.

But sometimes, women pounded the dried food to make **meal**. Then, they put the meal in a basket and mixed it with water to make soup. To heat the soup, they placed hot stones inside the basket.

**A bola was made of cord with weights attached to both ends. When a hunter threw a bola at a bird, it wrapped around the animal. Then, its weights dragged the bird to the ground.**

9

# Homes

The Modoc lived in two types of homes. During the winter, they lived in earthen lodges. In the summer or while traveling, they lived in smaller, dome-shaped homes. Usually, one family lived in each home.

Earthen lodges were circular and measured between 15 and 40 feet (5 and 12 m) across the middle. They were built partly underground, over a pit that was 3 to 4 feet (1 to 1.2 m) deep.

The Modoc used wooden posts and beams to form the frame of the lodge. They enclosed the frame with a layer of brush and **tule** mats. Finally, they covered the mats with dirt. These layers protected and warmed the lodge.

Each lodge had an opening in the center of the roof. Families used this opening to enter or exit the home. At the bottom of each home was a fire pit. The Modoc often built fires for cooking and warmth. Along the walls, there were beds made from tule mats. They were covered with blankets woven from plants or sewn from animal hides.

The Modoc made their summer homes, called wickiups, from **sapling** willow poles. To make the frame, they bent the poles and tied them together at the top. Then, they tied **tule** mats onto the frame. Some of these homes were as wide as ten feet (3 m) across the middle. But most of them were smaller.

The Modoc lived in both earthen lodges *(above)* and dome-shaped homes *(left)*. The underground dwellings kept the Modoc warm during cold winters.

11

# Clothing

The Modoc wore clothing made from plant fibers and animal hides. Typically, men wore shirts and leggings made from deer, elk, or antelope skins. Women wore dresses of the same materials.

During the summer, the Modoc did not wear much clothing. They wore only **breechcloths** or skirts made from **tule**. To protect their feet, they wore moccasins. Their summer moccasins were sewn from animal hides.

Both men and women wore robes over their clothing in the winter. They used rabbit skins, bird skins, or grass to weave the robes. People who were wealthy wore robes of elk or bobcat hides. The Modoc wore winter moccasins woven from tule. They also wore winter hats made of fur with flaps that covered the ears.

While working outdoors, the Modoc wore waterproof hats. These hats protected them from the sun and the rain. Men usually wore plain hats, and women wore hats woven with designs.

The Modoc often traded goods with neighboring tribes. In return, they received grass skirts, beads, and shells. They used the beads and shells to decorate clothing. And they used beads, wood, and bones to make necklaces.

**Before European influence, the Modoc wore clothing made from materials found in nature.**

# Crafts

The Modoc are known for their basketry. Elders passed on the art of basket making to younger generations. It took many years of practice to weave beautiful baskets.

The first step of the basket-weaving process was gathering the necessary materials. This was a fun social activity for the women. They talked with family and friends while collecting **tule**, willow shoots, and cattails.

When the women had gathered enough materials, they began to weave. They wove patterns of straight lines, squares, or triangles. To help them weave, they used bone **awls** and thread made from plant fibers.

Some baskets were woven so tight that they could hold water. The women coated these baskets with a waterproof substance. Then, they could use them to store water or cook food. Other baskets were designed specially for storing food.

Women made several different kinds of baskets for gathering food. Some were crafted to knock seed off grass. Others were used to carry food. These baskets had straps attached to them, so they were easy to carry. The women also made basket hats that they wore while gathering food.

Sometimes, women used natural dyes to color basket materials. They made the dyes from minerals and plants.

# Family

Modoc villages contained **extended families**. Family members helped with daily tasks to contribute to the success of their village. Tasks were handed out according to age. Elders often stayed in the village while younger people traveled. Usually, men and women had different responsibilities, too.

A man's primary responsibilities were hunting and fishing. Men were also in charge of making rafts and canoes for fishing. They made a raft from **tule**. To tie the pieces of tule together, the men used rope made from rolled plant fibers. They pushed the raft through the water with poles.

To make a dugout canoe, the men hollowed out the inside of a large pine or cedar tree. They used bone or stone tools to shape the canoe's exterior. Wooden paddles helped them push the canoe through the water.

Women were responsible for preparing hides, making clothing, and weaving baskets and blankets. To sew clothing, women used thread made from **sinew** or rolled plant fibers. But most important, women watched over the children and prepared food.

Modoc men worked hard to make dugout canoes. They used them to fish, gather food, and conduct trades.

17

# Children

The Modoc carried their babies in cradles woven from willow. A woven **tule** mattress was attached to the frame. Babies were not named until they were one year old.

As they grew, Modoc children learned important things from the elders. They learned how to act morally in their society. And they learned traditional songs, dances, and stories. Both boys and girls helped with daily work, such as gathering food. And, men and women taught them the tasks that boys and girls were expected to learn.

Men taught the boys how to hunt and fish. Sometimes, a deer hunter wore a deer hide to disguise himself. This fooled the animal and allowed the hunter to get close enough to kill it. Boys learned how to disguise themselves and quietly walk into a herd of deer.

Women showed girls where to find tule and willow for weaving. The art of weaving took many years to develop. But by the age of 12, most girls could make respectable baskets.

Modoc children used digging sticks and special baskets to help the women collect seed.

19

# Myths

Native American tribes pass on special stories, or myths. These myths allow us to learn about tribal **cultures** and traditions. The following Modoc myth explains how people arrived on Earth.

Long ago, an old man and his daughter were the only living beings on Earth. After a while, the old man became lonely. So, the two of them traveled to the Spirit World. There, they could visit the spirits.

When they arrived, they found themselves surrounded by skeletons. But during the night, the bones turned into humans and began to sing and dance! The old man and his daughter enjoyed their company. It made them feel less lonely. But when the sun rose, the humans turned back into skeletons.

The old man decided to bring the skeletons to Earth. He wanted to populate the world. So, he put them in a large basket and tied it onto his back for the journey home. When he reached Earth, he pulled out the bones. As he tossed them into the air, they magically became humans again.

The old man created different Native American tribes. He told the Modoc that although they were few, they would be a strong-spirited tribe. When the old man had completed his work on Earth, he and his daughter went to live in the sky. This is where they still live today.

According to Modoc myth, an old man created humans from bones. He promised the Modoc that he would teach special men how to become good leaders.

# War

Keeping peaceful relations with neighbors and visitors was important to the Modoc. But sometimes peace efforts failed. When this happened, the Modoc were prepared to fight. They wanted to protect their people and lands.

The Modoc were respected warriors. War leaders carefully planned out attacks. Prior to battle, the tribe held ceremonies to prepare themselves for fighting. Sometimes, a shaman performed during these ceremonies. The Modoc believed that a shaman's influence would protect the warriors and bring them victories.

The warriors wore armor to protect themselves. The Modoc made body armor from serviceberry rods. They used cords to weave the rods together. And, they used two layers of elk hide to make helmets. To disguise themselves, they wore sagebrush in their hair.

Modoc warriors fought with knives, spears, clubs, and bows and arrows. Knives were made from **obsidian**, bones, or antlers.

Clubs and bows and arrows were made from wood. Arrow tips were also made from **obsidian**.

However, all of these weapons were no match when fighting against the Europeans. So after the Modoc began trading with the Europeans, they also used guns during war.

**Modoc warriors wore armor made from serviceberry rods. Serviceberry is a tree or a shrub that produces white flowers and fruit.**

# Contact with Europeans

European fur traders made contact with the Modoc in the 1820s. But the Modoc were wary of them. The tribe saw the Europeans as a threat to their strong trade relations with neighboring tribes.

Around 1850, Europeans invaded Modoc territory. They wanted to settle Modoc land and search for gold. Unfortunately, their presence scared away many animals. This made food scarce for the Modoc. And, many Modoc died from European illnesses such as smallpox. During this time, the Modoc population was quickly reduced.

In 1864, a Modoc leader named Old Schonchin signed a treaty. The document forced the Modoc to live with the Klamath, a tribe that was once an enemy. The two tribes shared a **reservation** in Oregon on traditional Klamath land.

The Klamath treated the Modoc as intruders. And, food was limited on the reservation. This caused many people to become ill. Most Modoc were unhappy there. They asked for a separate reservation, but the federal government did not permit this.

In the late 1800s, many Modoc embraced the Ghost Dance religion. They believed it would bring back their dead ancestors and restore their traditional ways of life. To perform the Ghost Dance ceremony, the Modoc painted their faces red and drew two black lines on each cheek. Then, they held hands and danced around a fire.

The U.S. government pressured Old Schonchin to sign a treaty. The agreement forced the Modoc to share a reservation with the Klamath.

# Kintpuash

Kintpuash (KIHNT-pooahsh) was a famous Modoc leader. He was born around 1837. European settlers called him "Captain Jack." Like many other Modoc, Kintpuash was unhappy living on the **reservation**. He longed to return to his tribal homelands. So in 1870, he led a group of Modoc back to their territory.

Kintpuash's group set up a village along the Lost River. However, the European settlers demanded that the group leave. So in 1872, the federal government sent troops to force the Modoc off the land. Some Modoc refused, which started the Modoc War.

To escape, Kintpuash led about 80 warriors and their families to hiding spots. They hid in deep lava channels and caves for nearly one year. These areas provided a quick escape and allowed the Modoc to secretly plan attacks. Because of this, the Modoc won battles even though they were outnumbered.

In April 1873, Kintpuash had a peace meeting with government representatives. But the meeting was far from peaceful. With pressure mounting from his followers, Kintpuash killed Brigadier General Edward Canby during their meeting.

Two months later, a follower of Kintpuash betrayed him. He showed the government troops the Modoc hideouts. Kintpuash and his group surrendered. On October 3, Kintpuash and three Modoc warriors were put to death. The rest of his group was sent to a **reservation** in present-day Oklahoma.

**To avoid living on a reservation, Kintpuash and other Modoc hid in lava channels and caves. Today, this area is known as "Captain Jack's Stronghold."**

 # The Modoc Today

In 1909, some Modoc returned to the **reservation** in Oregon. Others remained in Oklahoma. To survive, the Modoc had to adopt European ways of life. In the process, they lost much of their traditional **culture**.

In 1978, **descendants** of the Modoc that had remained in Oklahoma became **federally recognized**. They are known as the Modoc Tribe of Oklahoma. This tribe is located in Miami, Oklahoma, where the Modoc tribal building also stands. The building holds the tribal headquarters, library, and historical records.

The Modoc Tribe of Oklahoma and the Miami Nation of Oklahoma co-own a restaurant and other businesses. **Revenue** from these businesses supports Modoc programs and services. These include housing improvement, child welfare, and environmental protection programs. The Modoc tribe also offers emergency medical and parenting support services.

In 2000, almost 480 Americans claimed full Modoc ancestry. And 960 claimed part Modoc ancestry. The Modoc continue to pass on their cultural traditions. People, such as Modoc tribal historian Patricia Scruggs Trolinger, work hard to teach others about the tribe's history and culture.

The Modoc continue to make baskets today. Traditional basket weavers still teach the skill to others. Some baskets are displayed in museums so that people can learn about Native American crafts and basketry.

Today, people can visit Captain Jack's Stronghold (above). There, visitors can trace the paths that the Modoc walked years ago when Kintpuash led them into hiding.

Modoc Bill Hayes (right) is dressed in traditional dance clothing. He is ready to compete at a powwow.

# Glossary

**awl** - a pointed tool for making small holes in materials such as leather or wood.

**breechcloth** - a piece of hide or cloth, usually worn by men, that wraps between the legs and ties with a belt around the waist.

**butte** - a lone, steep hill with a flat top.

**culture** - the customs, arts, and tools of a nation or people at a certain time.

**descendant** - a person who comes from a particular ancestor or group of ancestors.

**dialect** - a form of a language spoken in a certain area or by certain people.

**extended family** - a family that includes grandparents, uncles, aunts, and cousins in addition to a mother, father, and children.

**federal recognition** - the U.S. government's recognition of a tribe as being an independent nation. The tribe is then eligible for special funding and for protection of its reservation lands.

**meal** - coarsely ground seed.

**migrate** - to move from one place to another, often to find food.

**obsidian** - a hard, glassy rock formed when lava cools.

**plateau** - a raised area of flat land.

**reservation** - a piece of land set aside by the government for Native Americans to live on.

**revenue** - the total income produced from a given source.

**sapling** - a young tree.

**sinew** - a band of tough fibers that joins a muscle to a bone.

**tule** - a type of reed that grows in wetlands. Tule is native to California.

# Web Sites

To learn more about the Modoc, visit ABDO Publishing Company on the World Wide Web at **www.abdopublishing.com**. Web sites about the Modoc are featured on our Book Links page. These links are routinely monitored and updated to provide the most current information available.

# Index